HOW TO CHOOSE DRESS COLORS FOR LOVE AND SUCCESS

The CAANS System

Jim Andersen

HOW TO CHOOSE DRESS COLORS FOR
LOVE AND SUCCESS
The CAANS System
© By Ashok Malhotra, February 2014
Revision September 16, 2014

Quesst Publications

ISBN-13: 978-1495971419
By CreateSpace
USA

Jim Andersen is a pen name

Contents

THE CAANS SYSTEM

1

Introduction

You may have noticed how attractive that special person in your life looked while wearing a dress of a certain color or conversely, how drab he or she looked in another color. The colors of a dress we wear not only influence how we feel and behave but also influence those who interact with us.

Dress Colors and Human personality

This book deals with very one very specific and narrow aspect of human personality – the choice of dress colors. Human personalities have a huge depth and breadth. Let us consider where the choice of dress color fits in. For ease of understanding, consider the human personality at five levels. The deepest level of personality is a place from where arises consciousness, the freedom to choose, our desires, aversions and emotions. It is what some call the soul.

It is the core of our being and undoubtedly the most influential aspect of our personalities. At the next level are our thoughts and thought processes. The third level of personality is our physical selves that include our physical make up. At the fourth level we have external aspects of our personality that include mannerisms including how we speak, walk, talk, look etc. To these four levels of personality humans have added yet one more. This includes grooming, cleanliness, and dress. This external layer is in a sense like the cover of a huge book and just as a book is first judged by its covers, a human too makes his or her first impression by dress and external appearance.

In the pursuit of improving personality, one may say that while external appearance may be improved within a matter of hours, the next level that include mannerisms can also be improved through a training program of a few weeks. The third level i.e. health can be improved in a matter of months through a regimen of carefully selected diet, exercise and discipline. It goes without saying that for these changes to become a habit and a permanent part of personality, they have to be kept up over long periods of time. The potential for improvement is limited by natural abilities. For example a person who is physically handicapped will remain so. A person who walks with a stoop can be taught to walk straight with practice but a person with a physical hunchback cannot. A person who tends to look sideways with a tilted head may be taught to hold his head straight and look straight ahead but a person with a squint cannot do that. Nevertheless, each personality may improve within constraints of natural limitation through effort, training and practice. It is worth making that effort because everything we achieve in life is a result of our personality.

Thought processes arise from yet deeper levels of personality and cannot be improved in a matter of weeks or months but may certainly be improved over the years through education. However, when it comes to yet deeper emotional levels that are at the root of personality, change may take decades, even lifetimes. Changes come about simply through the experience of living. Practices such as meditation and reflection may hasten this process. Inculcating values of love, truth and simplicity charge the soul of a human with joy and charm.

The question then arises, if external appearances are the least important why stress on that? The answer is simple - because it is the easiest and quickest to change, this is where change must begin. First impressions open doors. One may never open a book with a poor cover and there are very many situations in life where first impression may be the only one. This is where a dress in the proper style and color comes in. When it comes to choice of dress colors, the right ones make us feel and behave better and also makes others we interact with behave with us differently. Maintained over long periods, the right appearance strengthens our inner positive side.

Dress Color

As in everything else in life, there is the middle and moderate road as regards external appearance and there is the extreme one too. An extreme way to attract attention for a man would be to walk about town with his trousers unzipped and his penis sticking out, if one may quote a rather extreme example. However such a way to attract attention is not only socially unacceptable and gross, it is also illegal in most parts of the world. While exposing oneself is illegal, there are other ways in which some humans may attract attention that are in some sense equally gross but not illegal, as for example massive tattoos, pins and needles on their faces, strange hair styles etc. for example colored orange and rising up like a flame on the nut. All of these extreme measures may attract temporary attention but they do not produce lasting gain. Successful persons do not use such extreme measures. Moderation is the route to success in life as far as appearances go. It is true that there may be a situation where an unusual appearance is proper but such as these latter are best affected through temporary changes. Thus while a flag painted on the face for a football match may be washed off later, a tattoo cannot be removed easily.

Returning to the topic of this book, dress colors, a similar logic applies. Fortunately dress is something that does not stick permanently to ones body and therefore one may keep a few items in ones wardrobe for that special occasion while pursuing moderation in one's daily wear. While one would like to maintain moderation in dress, most humans would also like to assert their individuality through a unique signature of dress colors that is effective for their personality and helps to add charm and enhance it. It is from this point of view that recommendations have been developed for this book.

Dress colors change with time and culture but what is proposed in this book are the best available standards of our present day world with reference to the best international benchmarks. The standard colors as acceptable for men and women that are neutral and not personality dependent are described in this small book in keeping with modern sensibilities. Next a couple of unique colors that vary with individuals and are specific for each person are also described through the present system named as CAANS so that one may then proceed to design one's wardrobe in colors that are not only the most appropriate ones but also make one look more attractive and as a result more successful in life as compared to one going about in the wrong or safe colors. Aside from benefits to an individual, society as a whole benefits when people dress in colors that enhance love, peace, tranquility, beauty and happiness rather than others that may assault and jar the senses or conversely are drab and depressing like that dull gray day when one is left wishing for the sun.

Every human personality is unique. Even identical twins have their unique personalities because each undergoes different experiences from the moment of conception. Therefore, there are different and unique colors of dress for each person that will bring out the best in them on any given occasion. How do we find out what this color is? Some of us probably already know, based on our own experience in life. Perhaps, those who cared told us how beautiful and dashing we looked in a tie, shirt, scarf or dress of a certain color. However, many of us may not have made this discovery yet. We may not have even tried wearing that particular colored dress that is special to us. This book attempts to outline a new method of discovering those colors while also elaborating on modern dress colors that are applicable to all.

Men and women who have discovered their personal colors look more confident and more attractive. It is not surprising if they tend to be more successful in life as compared to others who have not yet made this discovery. Appropriate colors make you look healthier, younger, energetic, and happier and when it comes to success there is nothing like happiness to attract it. The right choice of dress color is a must for those looking for greater love, success and happiness in their lives.

How much and what part of your dress should be in selected colors and when to wear it is a separate issue. First of all, when it comes to work, certain dress colors are customary. There may be a prescribed uniform for work or a religious order and the color is therefore predefined during work hours. Even if a uniform is not predefined, it is customary for professional executives to wear a white shirt. White is a mixture of all colors and most conducive for efficiency and portraying the right impression at work. It compliments all other colors. However executives have flexibility in choosing the color of their tie and it would be smart for an executive to wear the right colored tie frequently at work. While modern men know that it is acceptable to wear a tie of any color, it does not mean that every color is as effective for a tie. The CAANS system described in this book throws up new unique suggestions for each person.

For men engaged in the arts and entertainment industry, white is often not suitable since their role in life is to perpetuate relaxation rather than work discipline and for those engaged in manual labor white is impractical. On the other hand, women have a greater flexibility in choice of their dress colors but not all colors are best in a work environment. In this case one may choose a scarf, jewelry or dress top in the suggested CANNS color only unless it turns out to be safe one, but when it comes to that special dinner meeting or date, a lady may go all the way and have a full length gown or dress in her favorite color. Similarly when away from work, it would be smart for men to wear a shirt, jacket or pullover of a color that brings out the best in them in a social way.

When the right colors are found, it is advantageous to wear it near the face and heart because it is here that the aura of a human is strongest and it is here that colors influence most. Much more flexibility can be used for the dress on the lower half of the body except for certain purposes such as lustful pursuits touched upon in a later section. However, as mentioned earlier, if it is an evening gown for a lady, a single color for an entire dress would be most harmonious. As regards men, a single color for all items of dress may become clownish rather than elegant unless it is a religious robe, ceremonial or ritualistic dress.

When a dress consists of more than one color, care is required that a combination does not have an undesirable impact. Thus, whereas it is regarded safe for men to wear trousers and jackets in shades of gray and blue with a white shirt at work (Brown is for Sundays, if at all) the color combinations that can be worn by women are much larger simply because their choice of dress colors is vast. Care is required by ladies that a right effect is created in their choice of color combinations from the range of choices available to them. Certain colors such as white and black are neutral and combine with most colors harmoniously. However care is required in using black. Certain color combinations e.g. red and black that are often employed for commercial purposes, appeal to baser human instincts. It may produce temporary commercial gain but may leave the one who wears it depressed. In mythology ancient seers have used this color combination to depict the devil. Different colors, when side by side take on an entirely new meaning like words do in different sentences, a meaning that is quickly discerned by mystic seers who specialize more in the language of emotions rather than the mind.

The present system of color selection called the CAANS system suggests a set of complimentary shades that may be combined with a primary selection to create dress ensembles. CAANS is abbreviation for: Computer Aided Astro Numerological Selection. While much that is frequently dished out under the name of Para normal sciences does appear to be irrelevant, there is also some that has been a part of human belief systems for thousands of years. It is worth approaching these with an open mind so that potential benefits, if any, are not missed especially when there is nothing much to lose in doing so. Mystic insights of genuine seers, unhindered by a necessity of scientific validation have been valued by humans from the beginning of human civilization.

There is undoubtedly much that still remains beyond the reach of scientific understanding. For example, in the area of clothing colors, many have realized that professional executives appear and behave far more efficiently in a white shirt and navy blue jacket rather than in a dark shirt and brown jacket and ladies in scarlet are far more vibrant than others in dull gray. Kings and queens have used dress color effectively since the beginning of history to assert their influence, not just in clothes but also in the jewels they wore. It seems that one of the most beautiful queens in all of history, Cleopatra, frequently wore a broad necklace of closely set blue lapis lazuli and turquoise around her neck even when she wore not much else.

In the present system named as CAANS, fundamental empirical knowledge of influence of color on human behavior has been combined with basic aspects of empirical knowledge from areas of astrology and numerology. For example, astrology has claimed that planet mars has a greater influence on persons born under the sun sign of Aries rather than other signs. Further, it has been the experience of this author that certain numbers repeatedly play a fortunate or unfortunate role in life as has been the experience of very many other sensitive humans and that in some way these numbers appear to be connected with one's date of birth. Starting with such elementary aspects of numerology and astrology the CAANS system was gradually built up, initially as just an exercise for fun rather than anything more serious. However, as results emerged that appeared highly effective the author has decided to share the method in a systematic and easily understood manner through this brief book. A wider application of the method will reveal its further usefulness. The author would appreciate if readers share their views on it for others as online comments, perhaps at a location from where they first heard of this book, so that the CAANS system can be developed further, if required. An explanation of how these numbers were arrived at is presently withheld as a secret.

As mentioned, the method suggested in the present booklet discovers just two colors for most persons. However, when added to a set of complimentary colors or shades the selection becomes large. Depending upon the occasion, a person could combine these selected colors in a suitable manner for a dress. One may consult fashion experts if one has easy access to them or friends and associates who have a good dress sense to decide what precise combinations to use. While consulting others, it may be mentioned that older persons, especially those who have been around and are social and loving personalities, make much better consultants than younger friends.

It may be observed that tribal persons are fond of wearing clothing printed with large floral or geometric motifs. However as humans get more sophisticated, their taste in clothing changes to finer prints and eventually solid colors. Once one has narrowed down the range of colors that are most suitable for each individual, the long road to choosing one's wardrobe is much easier. What are the tools available to any person to discover their most advantageous personal colors? Three methods, either in isolation or combination have been used often for the purpose

- The choice of dress color is most simply decided based on custom and availability. The choice may be based on personal experience that includes recommendation of those who love us or by preference and taste. It may be mentioned that whereas taste is a good guide when it comes to select food, it is not such a good one when it comes to choosing dress color. Persons sometimes choose a dress color that looked fantastic on someone else without realizing that it does not work for them, or they may choose a color to try and become a personality they are not. It does not work because the best approach is to be true to oneself.

- The choice of dress color is decided by consulting a fashion or dress expert. Fashion experts can help choose dress colors based on your skin tone, hair color etc. and what is trending. However, they may not know about your inner personality and what is best for you.
- The color is discovered through astrological, numerological, psychic or mystical insights. These last can not be proven by science but then science fails when it comes to proving anything in the realm of emotions. There are many humans who have claimed that they have benefited by such advice.

When dress colors are decided on the basis of custom, these tend to change with time and the colors so selected may be a reflection of the times rather than the most conducive ones. Ancient astrological science has methods for recommending dress colors based on one's astrological charts or sun signs but the recommendations are limited simply because colors could be defined only in a limited way in the past.

Color Psychology

Color psychology is the study of how color influences human behavior. However, the interface between color and environmental stimuli is a highly complex interface and influence of a color can vary in different cultures and with different persons. The same color can create a different emotion in different circumstances and in combination with other colors. Following are some of the common emotions associated with colors but as mentioned they are only an approximate indication. The psychological impact of color changes with context.

Red: Lust, Negativity, Excitement, Love

Red is a powerful color. It has the longest wavelength of colors in the visible range. It grabs our attention quickly and is therefore used as a color of warning and traffic lights. It stimulates us and raises the pulse rate, giving the impression that time is passing faster than it is. Pure red is the simplest color, with no subtlety. It is stimulating and lively, very friendly. At the same time, it can be demanding and aggressive.

Yellow: Jealousy, Competence, Happiness

The right shade yellow will produce happiness. It is the color of confidence and optimism. However the wrong shade of it can produce the opposite effect.

Orange: Warmth, security, fun

Being a combination of red and yellow it is the combination of excitement and happiness i.e. fun

Green: Envy, Security

Green is in the centre of the spectrum. It is the color of balance. When the world about us contains plenty of green, this indicates the presence of water and food producing a sense of security.

Blue: Masculine, Competence, High Quality, Corporate

Being the color of sky and clear waters, blue is a peaceful and soothing color. It stimulates clear thinking and light blues calm the mind. However, it can also be perceived as cold, and unfriendly.

Pink: Sophistication, sincerity, grace

Pink is a lighter tint of red but unlike red it soothes rather than excite. It represents the feminine principle, it is nurturing and compassionate.

Violet/purple: Authority, Power, sophistication

It is the shortest wavelength. It takes awareness to a higher level of thought, even into spiritual values. It encourages deep contemplation and meditation. It has also been associated with royalty and therefore also conveys authority.

Brown: Ruggedness, contentment

Brown is the colors of the earth and the natural world. It is a solid, reliable color and most people find it quietly supportive. It also denotes relaxation and inertia and therefore it is not dynamic for men's clothing unless for a visit to the temple or a holiday.

Gray: Conservatism, dependability, depressing

Gray is the only color that has no direct psychological properties. It however denotes dependability, especially when worn on the lower part of a male body. On the upper part of the body it is depressing as when the world turns gray unless over a white or another color shirt.

Black: Grief, Fear, Elegance, sophistication

Black is absence of light, since no wavelengths are reflected and it can therefore be menacing on the negative side. Positively, it communicates absolute clarity and sophistication, and uncompromising excellence.

White: purity, sincerity, peace, truthfulness

White is a mixture of all colors and the purest of them all. It conveys no negative emotion and is therefore a safe color in dress for both men and women.

With new information technology, a vast range of colors can be defined with precision. This is what has been done in this book so that a person is able to find a dress color that fits their unique personality.

Based on simple information personal to you, personality types have been classified into more than 9000 different types and a simple method has been suggested to choose a color for that personality type from amongst thousands of possible colors. It is hoped that these big numbers do not intimidate you because selection is really simple, once you learn the technique by reading the pages of this brief booklet. An elementary knowledge of use of a personal computer is required and if the reader has not acquired that, one can easily ask someone to display your color on a personal computer once you have defined its RGB values. Let us consider these in the next chapter.

"It is not expensive clothes that are necessarily nice but clothes that are clean and in the right colors that are nice"

2
Defining Color

Color or color is the perception capacity of humans. Color arises because of the spectrum of light in which each color of light has a certain wavelength that interacts with the eye and the spectral sensitivities of light receptors within it. Color categories and physical specifications of color are also associated with objects or materials based on their physical properties such as light absorption, reflection, or emission spectra. Because perception of color stems from varying spectral sensitivity of different types of cone cells in the retina to different parts of the spectrum, colors may be defined and quantified by the degree to which they stimulate these cells. These physical or physiological quantifications of color, however, do not fully explain the psychophysical and psychological perception of color.

The science of color is sometimes called chromatics or simply color science. It includes the perception of color by the human eye and brain, the origin of color in materials, color theory, art, design, fashion and the science of radiation in the visible range, the range we call light.

The color of an object depends on both the object and its environment. It also depends on the characteristics of the perceiving eye and brain. Physically, objects can be said to have the color of the light leaving their surfaces. Some objects not only reflect light, but also transmit light or emit light themselves, which also adds to the color. A viewer's perception of the object's color depends not only on the spectrum of the light leaving its surface, but also on a host of other cues, so that color differences between objects can be defined independent of the lighting spectrum, viewing angle, etc.

Aristotle and other ancient scientists had already written on the nature of light and color. However, it was not until Isaac Newton that light was identified as the source of the color sensation. In 1810, Goethe published his comprehensive theory in which he ascribed physiological effects to color. In 1801 Thomas Young proposed his theory of three colors based on the observation that any color could be matched with a combination of three lights. This theory was later refined by other scientists. In 1931, an international group of experts known as the CIE developed a mathematical color model, which mapped out the space of observable colors and assigned a set of three numbers to each.

The ability of the eye to distinguish colors is based upon the varying sensitivity of different cells in the human retina to light of different wavelengths. Human retina contains three types of color receptor cells, or cones. Light, no matter how complex its composition of wave length is reduced to three color components by the eye. For each location in the visual field, the three types of cones yield three signals based on the extent to which each is stimulated. However, when these signals reach the brain they can stimulate a range of experiences that depends not just on the color but also the personality of the one perceiving it.

Although there are individual differences in personalities, large groups of humans within a community share certain common traits and it is because of this that one may venture into something like the science of dress color. Nevertheless, these common traits vary with time and place and it is because of this that some colors that were thought to be fashionable at one time are no more so.

Specifying Color

A color can be specified by specifying the intensity of its three components – red, green and blue. When you assign a value between zero and 255 to each of these colors and combine them, a color is created that is defined by these RGB values. If you are familiar with use of a word processor then it is easy to see what any combination of R, G and B leads to. Let us try by writing the letter A and then assigning it a color with

R=150
G=50
B=25

To do this type out the letter A in a large font size and then select a custom color for it with these values. It will lead to a shade of brown,

To get the letter A in this color we selected the font to be of size 72 and then clicked on an icon in the tool bar at top to choose color. A palette of colors was displayed with forty pre-selected colors but there was an icon below the palette that said more colors and a further choice to specify a custom color was revealed. Clicking on the custom color option revealed a new window with a table in which we could fill in our chosen values to reveal the color.

Let us try another example with a different choice of RGB. Let,

R=10
G=100
B =200

Now let us repeat the exercise with coloring the letter A with these values and we get a shade of blue,

Let us try a third example with

R=100
G=100
B=100
The resulting color is

That is a very dark shade of gray. Had we pushed up our selection of RGB to 250 each, the color would have become pure white. If the color selected is a very light, near white color, it can be displayed better by filling a rectangle or ellipse with that custom color. This too is done easily in a word processor program. You may wonder what happens to the color if RGB are all made zero

R=0
G=0
B=0

Now we shall end up with black as below

A

Thus it is possible to define a color with its RGB values and that is how we shall define your favorite color once it has been ascertained.

It is all right to give a name to a color when one is dealing with just a few colors, but when one has thousands of colors to deal with, the RGB code is the easiest route to follow and that is the route we shall follow to define color based on basic information such as your name and date of birth while using the simplest of techniques from astrology, numerology and mystic insights. However the book contains an appendix from where you can find out the name of the color too if you wish, at least approximately.

~

3
Discovering Your Colors

The procedure that has been followed in the present methodology is to select individual R, G and B values of your personal colors based on some critical information personal to you. No one else need know this information since you can make the discovery in the privacy of your home by yourself after reading this chapter. Let us begin with the R digit

R Value

In order to know your R value the first step is to determine your astrological sun sign and assign its corresponding R value for the present system. Your sun sign considers the position of Sun at birth within the twelve Zodiac sun signs. Referring to the table you may easily determine your sun sign. Those born in the cusp, that is plus minus three days of the terminal date would bear some personality characteristics of the adjoining sun sign, more so because these are approximate dates and can vary by a day or two. Therefore they would get an opportunity to select a secondary R value based on that sun sign and thus be able to find two colors that are personal to them.

Table of Sun Sign dates

Sign names	Dates
Capricorn	December 22 – January 20
Aquarius	January 21 – February 18
Pisces	February 19 – March 19
Aries	March 20 – April 19
Taurus	April 20 – May 20
Gemini	May 21 – June 20
Cancer	June 21 – July 22
Leo	July 23 – August 22
Virgo	August 23 – September 22
Libra	September 23 – October 22
Scorpio	October 23 – November 21
Sagittarius	November 22 – December 21

Table of R Value

Sign names	R Value
Capricorn	200
Aquarius	230
Pisces	245
Aries	250
Taurus	240
Gemini	220
Cancer	175
Leo	125
Virgo	50
Libra	0
Scorpio	100
Sagittarius	150

Just look up the table and make a note of your R value on a piece of paper. Finding the other two G and B values will be just as simple and that is an exercise one has to do before one can define a color.

G Value

The G value is selected based on numerological consideration of your day of birth. It is given in the following table. Just the date is required, not the year or month here.

Table of G Values

Date	G Value
1	200
2	220
3	150
4	200
5	220
6	200
7	175
8	50
9	200
10	220
11	220
12	150
13	125

14	240
15	200
16	175
17	100
18	200
19	200
20	175
21	150
22	250
23	220
24	200
25	175
26	230
27	200
28	220
29	200
30	245
31	175

B Value

Just one more field of definition remains to specify a color, the B value. This field has been defined with the help of the first letter of a name. The first letter of a name has considerable astrological and personal influence according to ancient Sanskrit literature. Astrologers in the east often try to harmonize names with the astrological chart at birth but that practice has more or less disappeared with time. In the CAANS system, it has been connected to blue component of color in and RGB code. The values for each starting alphabet of a name are listed below. To discover these values a far greater effort was required than in discovering the other fields. Initially a value for X eluded the author but since there are names that begin with this letter in some countries, a greater effort was made and finally that too was found. The existing practice of connecting names to a number in series as in numerology was found inadequate particularly because of the apparent random order in which the English alphabet is arranged unlike in Sanskrit. It is not possible to record the full methodology here since it involves meditative practices that in any case would not be understandable to many. The full set is listed in the table.

Once you have found the RGB values you might wish to know the name of the color. Do look up Appendix for that and look for one that comes close.

Table of B Values

Letter	B Value
A	100
B	150
C	240
D	230
E	220
F	150
G	220
H	150
I	230
J	240
K	175
L	175
M	125
N	150
O	220
P	125
Q	200
R	100
S	220
T	50
U	200
V	175
W	150
X	175
Y	200
Z	200

Illustrations

Let us illustrate the present method by an example from a famous couple, Angelina Jolie and Brad Pitt.
Angelina was born on June 4, 1975. Therefore by referring to the preceding tables her R value corresponding to the Gemini sun sign is 220, the G value corresponding to her birthday of 4th is 200 and the B value corresponding to the first letter of her name A is 100. The corresponding color filled in a figure drawn in word 2003 is

The RGB values of Brad Pitt on the other hand corresponding to his birthday of December 18 are 150, 200, and 150 by reference to tables. The same figure filled with these colors is

Wonder if the two have tried these colors. Worn together at the same time, it would be a dashing couple indeed, Angelina with a full length dress of her color and brad with just a shirt in it with blue jeans, black or gray trouser. The colors chosen by the present system are often not striking ones like shocking pink that might make a strong first impression but not a lasting and durable one.

Let us now consider the color for Queen Elizabeth born on April 21 1926. Her R, G, B values are 240, 150 and 220 respectively and the corresponding color is,

The color is indeed dashing and of a royal hue of pink, very appropriate for the most famous Queen of the modern world.

Let us next consider the color for Oprah Winfrey born on January 29. Her RGB values from the tables are: R 230 G 200 B 220 and the color ellipse filled with this color is

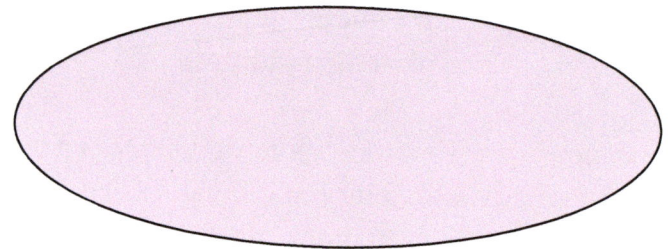

A Fashion expert may have chosen a darker color to match with her skin tone but this color would be rather becoming on her in keeping with her exuberant personality

Let us conclude with a famous personality of our times, President Barack Obama. He was born on August 4, 1961. His RGB values from the CANNS system are:

R=125

G =200

B =150

And his color filled in a rectangle is

That is a pleasant shade of Green for a weekend or evening shirt or perhaps a tie on a white shirt in work settings. The color has a regal touch to it that perhaps a US President does have because of the power he enjoys in his individual capacity, albeit for limited terms. Wonder if he knows about this color? In any case readers of this book can find out their shades now and even some complimentary ones as described in the next chapter. Once you have learnt this system, not only can you find your own color but also of others, especially persons who are important to you in life. It also shortens the task of selecting a gift for someone, if it is an item of clothing, easier.

The Second Color

A second color is suggested by CAANS that is based entirely on your birthday and does not include the name. It has a fundamental astro-numerological influence and is just as effective as the color that includes the name. It is found simply by making the B value in the previous selection equal to 250 or 255. These changes would not produce a dramatic color change for some whose name is already compatible with their other astro-numerological values but for others, the change may be dramatic. We shall discuss more about this in the next chapter when we consider the full range of dress colors a person may choose from. But as simple example consider the letter A with values of RGB equal to 180, 230, 70

Now let us make the value of B in the previous selection as 250 to yield RGB of 180, 230, 250

The color has changed to a shade of blue and led to a completely new color here.

4

Colors of Lust

Throughout this brief booklet it was stressed that it is clothing on the upper part of the body is most influential. However, there is an aspect of life where clothing on the lower part is even more important and this area is concerning matters of Lust. If it was not described earlier in the book, it was because the primary concern of this book was love rather than lust. Nevertheless, there are times when lust is important too. It is a necessity towards procreation and either way it dominates human thought even more than in the thoughts of lower animals that do it by the seasons.

In a sense, lust especially when it is purely physical negates love because ancient mystics have stated, where there is love there is no lust and where there is lust, there is no love. Lust opposes love just as darkness opposes light but as mentioned, since it has a role in life, this book would be incomplete without mentioning the colors associated with it, a color suitable for the lower half of a human body e.g. the underwear worn on that part.

The colors of lust are easily found by subtracting previously determined RGB values each from 250 for that value. Using 255 would be more accurate but for simplicity we choose 250 here since it does not make a discernible difference in the selection.

As an illustration, let us conclude this section in a lighter vein by revisiting the example for President Obama. It would not be polite to publish such details for the ladies but it is hoped that Barack Obama would be sporting about it. As described earlier his RGB values are

R=125
G =200
B =150

The color is suitable for a shirt, tie or Jacket. It is shown here again

Similarly the second CAANS color is (125,200,250)

The complimentary colors are
R= 250 -125 = 125
G =250 – 200 = 50
B = 250 -150 = 100

This last is then the suggested innerwear color in this last case for maximum impact. A second innerwear color may also be derived by using the second CAANS color similarly. It would have RGB values of 125. 50, 0 (by subtracting values from 250). It is a dark skin tone

-

5
A Palette of Complimentary Colors

Earlier chapters have helped define two personal dress colors based on name and date of birth. However, a wardrobe cannot be made up with just two colors. A much wider range is required to suit time and occasion and dresses are not always made of a single color. There is a need to combine it with other colors.

Let us consider complimentary colors. The CAANS system of color selection has discrete RGB values so that a finite number of colors can be worked with. This provides us with an opportunity to locate other suitable shades within the discrete range. Small changes of RGB values would not produce a discernible change but for some values a larger change is possible. If you locate that one of the RGB values is one of the numbers in the first column of the following table you may then choose the alternative suggestions to locate another shade that is equally valid and can be combined in a dress. However it must be pointed out that in many cases using alternative values may not make a discernible change in color, whereas in some cases it will.

Table of Alternative RGB Values

Original Value	Alternative Possible Values	
0	25	-
50	25	75
100	75	112
125	113	137
150	137	162
175	162	187
200	187	210

No alternative numbers are suggested for values above 200 because the CAANS system already defines values closely in that range. Aside from alternative shades that may be found in this manner, it must be mentioned that white is compatible with all colors since it is a mixture of all colors. It may be used liberally. Black too, as a color is compatible with all since it marks an absence of all light but it must be used with considerable care since it can also have a negative influence. Shades of Gray for trousers are neutral for men and may be combined with other colors of a shirt and jacket. Much more freedom may be exercised in choice of clothing for the lower half of a body as compared to upper half since it has much less influence on personality as compared to a color close to eyes, face and heart with the exception of certain areas of life as mentioned in the last chapter.

Once you have found a color on a computer screen, the task shall remain of making a copy of it on paper for you to carry to a store or dress maker. If one has access to a high quality color printer, one could make a copy. Some persons simply scan color magazines and try and match the shade to that in a magazine or book and use that as a sample. One could also try and get color charts of paint or dress makers and specify a shade through that. It must also be mentioned that slight variations from an actual shade are equally fortunate and are within the limits of accuracy of the CAANS process. How a color shows is also dependent on the fabric Shiny fabrics show the color more as compared to wool or cotton and it is appropriate to adjust the shade slightly so that it displays in the chosen shade from some distance in normal light.

White and Black

Aside from the astro-numerological colors described so far, there are some colors that are neutral and are compatible to all persons. They may have something with personality. First is pure white and the next is black. Near white shades such as ivory or other off whites have nearly the same property as regards dress.

Grays and Browns

Aside from the shades described thus far, there is a range of grays and browns that are neutral too. Grays ranging up to deep blue are neutral when worn on the lower half of a man's clothing or as a jacket over a white shirt. Brown is a neutral color for ladies in all its varied shades and ranges on the reddish side all the way up to scarlet red .

These latter shades may have something to do with skin, hair and eye tones but not so much with astronumerological factors. The use of these latter shades has varied with time. The present recommendation of this author is that men may choose additional dress items from a range of gray shades going up to dark blue and women from a range of browns up to scarlet for their dresses.

Brown shades are no longer recommended for men and gray no longer for women unless it happens to be a shade picked up by CAANS.

The precise shade of gray or brown that is selected, for a particular item of dress, cannot be prescribed here because it depends on skin, hair color tones etc. They would need to use their own experience and judgment for this or the opinion of friends or a stylist

HOW TO CHOOSE DRESS COLORS FOR LOVE AND SUCCESS

if accessible. The white and black shade is included in both tables too. However, one need not worry even if it is not the precise brown or gray shade that is chosen since all are fairly neutral and compatible.

The restriction for women not choosing gray shades is more severe then men not choosing browns. For informal and holiday wear a man may choose brown even though the recommendation of this book is that they are avoided.

Whereas a gray jacket over a white shirt is elegant in western dress, there is a different kind of jacket in South Asia that is closed at the neck so that the shirt does not show. In such cases, gray is not the best choice. It can be depressing without the benefit of a white shirt. South Asian men therefore often choose a brown jacket but as mentioned that too is not a good choice for men. A better choice is to use white, near white shades, black, dark blue or the one of the two CANNS colors. A jacket that consists of gray and white closely set thin stripes is also elegant where the white stripes play the same color role us a white shirt might.

Table- Tones of brown color for Women

Color		RGB
	White	250, 250,250
	Faded	250, 225, 200
	Tan:	210, 180, 140
	Pale Brown	152, 118, 84
	Russet	128, 70, 27
	Raw Umber	115, 74, 18
	Dark Brown	101, 67, 33
	Coffee	111, 78, 55
	Sepia	112, 66, 20
	Cafe Noir	75, 54, 33
	Black	0,0,0

Brown to Scarlet

	Brown	100, 50, 0
	Reddish Brown	150, 50, 0
	Earthy Red	200, 50, 0
	Scarlet	250, 50, 0

Table : Tones of gray color for Men

Color		RGB
	black	(0,0,0)
	Dark Gray	(75, 75,75)
	dim gray	(105,105,105)
	gray	(128,128,128)
	gray	(169,169,169)
	Silver gray	(192,192,192)
	light gray	(211,211,211)
	white smoke	(245,245,245)
	white	(250,250,250)

Blue to Gray

	Deep Blue	(0,0,140)
	Dark Blue Gray	(75, 75, 120)
	Dim Blue- gray	(105,105,120)
	Plain gray	(125,125,125)
	Dark Gray	(75, 75, 75)

Dress Color Palette

With the information given so far, we can now choose a complete color palette for every person consisting of the following colors:

1. White
2. Black
3. The CAANS system, first RGB Color
4. The second RGB color with B=250
5. Shades of Gray ranging up to dark blue chosen from the table for men, and shades of brown ranging up to scarlet for women

Thus both men and women have a fairly wide range of colors to choose from with their CAANS System colors providing a unique color signature to their choices. The given palette of dress colors makes the task of choosing dress colors much easier than it would otherwise be if one had to work with a palette of infinite colors where one is likely to go wrong.

A person's own dress sense is required to choose the right colors for each item of dress by their own experience, consultation with others and an observation of famous and successful personalities in the world. It is beyond the scope of this small book to go into the details of colors for each item of the dress. However a few hints can be included here. For example if one of the CAANS colors is a bright red for a man then it will be great to choose a white shirt, gray trouser, deep blue jacket and a red tie for work whereas the same person may wear a red shirt and a white tie at a party in the evening. Doing the reverse would be a disaster.

Just as the tie may be used to add color to a man's dress in a safe manner, jewelry and other accessories can do the same for women. Thus if a suggested color for a lady is emerald green she might choose this as the color of her jewelry to be worn with an elegant black evening gown. However for a morning dress to the market the entire dress may be in green or even a combination of green and white. Similarly if a CAANS color for a lady is brilliant pink it would not be the best thing to wear to the supermarket but a scarf of that color worn over a dull brown rain coat would be appropriate. For their informal day wear, ladies may choose some clothing printed in more than one color, although it is best to have most of the wardrobe in solid colors.

In conclusion it must be mentioned that once you discover your personal colors, you need not avoid other colors completely. All colors have a role to play just as all aspects of human behavior even some considered bad, are required in our journey through life, but the important thing is that you must be comfortable with the color and those who love you should be appreciative of it. There will be times and occasions when other colors will be required. However, to go into all of them would be beyond the scope of the present work. The CAANS system merely attempts to propose just two unique colors that are likely to be your most fortunate ones through most of your life when used along with other neutral colors as suitable for men and women in modern times. Once combined with other neutral shades, it would give you a spectrum of colors to design an entire wardrobe from.

This brings us to an end of the CAANS system of dress colors. This book is intentionally brief since its purpose is to introduce a new system and offer a quick guide rather than create a verbose book on colors of dress. Do try it and if you find it beneficial do let your friends know or post a review for the world because eventually most joy is added to one's life by sharing joy with others. Best wishes to the reader from the author in this exciting discovery.

APPENDIX – Names of Colors

RGB values are great to define colors but at times one wishes to find out to the name of a color. Following are some of the names. Perhaps you can find out the color you are looking for from RGB values or one close to it. The table was developed mostly from tables of colors on Wikipedia[1]

Table of some Colors

Color	R G B
Pink	255 192 203
Light Pink	255 182 193
Hot Pink	255 105 180
Deep Pink	255 20 147
Pale Violet Red	219 112 147
Medium Violet Red	199 21 133
Light Salmon	255 160 122
Salmon	250 128 114
Dark Salmon	233 150 122
Light Coral	240 128 128

[1] http://en.wikipedia.org/wiki/Web_colors

Indian Red	205 92 92
Crimson	220 20 60
Fire Brick	178 34 34
Dark Red	139 0 0
Red	255 0 0
Crimson	255 0 100
Tomato	255 99 71
Coral	255 127 80
Dark Orange	255 140 0
Orange	255 165 0
Yellow	255 255 0
Mustard Yellow	255 200 0
Light Yellow	255 255 224
Light Golden rod Yellow	250 250 210
Papaya Whip	255 239 213
Moccasin	255 228 181
Peach Puff	255 218 185
Pale Golden rod	238 232 170
Khaki	240 230 140

Dark Khaki	189 183 107
Gold	255 215 0
Corn silk	255 248 220
Blanched Almond	255 235 205
Navajo White	255 222 173
Wheat	245 222 179
Burly Wood	222 184 135
Tan	210 180 140
Rosy Brown	188 143 143
Sandy Brown	244 164 96
Golden rod	218 165 32
Peru	205 133 63
Chocolate	210 105 30
Saddle Brown	139 69 19
Sienna	160 82 45
Brown	150 50 0
Maroon	128 0 0
Dark Olive Green	85 107 47
Olive	128 128 0

Olive Drab	107 142 35
Yellow Green	154 205 50
Lime Green	50 205 50
Lime	0 255 0
Greenish Yellow	173 255 47
Spring Green	0 255 127
Medium Spring Green	0 250 154
Pale Green	152 251 152
Dark Sea Green	143 188 143
Medium Sea Green	60 179 113
Sea Green	46 139 87
Green	0 128 0
Dark Green	0 100 0
Medium Aquamarine	102 205 170
Aqua	0 255 255
Light Cyan	224 255 255
Pale Turquoise	175 238 238
Aquamarine	127 255 212
Turquoise	64 224 208

Medium Turquoise	72 209 204
Dark Turquoise	0 206 209
Light Sea Green	32 178 170
Cadet Blue	95 158 160
Teal	0 128 128
Light Steel Blue	176 196 222
Powder Blue	176 224 230
Light Blue	173 216 230
Sky Blue	135 206 235
Deep Sky Blue	0 191 255
Dodger Blue	30 144 255
Cornflower Blue	100 149 237
Steel Blue	70 130 180
Royal Blue	65 105 225
Blue	0 0 255
Medium Blue	0 0 205
Dark Blue	0 0 139
Navy	0 0 128
Midnight Blue	25 25 112

Lavender	230 230 250
Thistle	216 191 216
Plum	221 160 221
Violet	238 130 238
Orchid	218 112 214
Magenta	255 0 255
Medium Orchid	186 85 211
Medium Purple	147 112 219
Blue Violet	138 43 226
Dark Violet	148 0 211
Purple	128 0 128
Indigo	75 0 130
Dark Slate Blue	72 61 139
Slate Blue	106 90 205
Medium Slate Blue	123 104 238
White	255 255 255
Honey dew	240 255 240
Ghost White	248 248 255
White Smoke	245 245 245

Sea shell	255 245 238
Beige	245 245 220
Old Lace	253 245 230
Ivory	255 255 240
Antique White	250 235 215
Linen	250 240 230
Lavender Blush	255 240 245
Misty Rose	255 228 225
Gainesboro	220 220 220
Light Gray	211 211 211
Silver	192 192 192
Dark Gray	169 169 169
Gray	128 128 128
Dim Gray	105 105 105
Slate Gray	112 128 144
Dark Slate Gray	47 79 79
Deep Gray	50 50 50
Soft Black	25 25 25
Black	0 0 0

Suggestions for Further Reading

If you read the following books on the subject too, then you could become an expert on dress color and style as well, for both men and women.

Fashion in Costume, 1200-2000
By Nunn, Joan
Second edition, A & C Black (Publishers) Ltd; Chicago: New Amsterdam Books, 2000.

How to Dress for Success
By Edith Head
Abrams; Reprint edition (April 1, 2011)

John T. Molloy's New Dress for Success
Warner Books; Exp Updated edition (January 1, 1988)

Color Your Style: How to Wear Your True Colors
By David Zyla
Plume; 1ST edition (January 25, 2011)